RENA GLICKMAN,
QUEEN OF JUDO

For Pauline, amazing aunt, forever friend,
steadfast supporter —E.N.C.

Text copyright © 2022 by Eve Nadel Catarevas
Illustrations copyright © 2022 by Lerner Publishing Group, Inc.

KAR-BEN PUBLISHING®
An imprint of Lerner Publishing Group, Inc.
241 First Avenue North
Minneapolis, MN 55401 USA

Website address: www.karben.com

Photo credits: Photos courtesy of Jean Kanokogi, p. 32 (top right) (lower left); David Finch/Getty Images, p. 32 (lower right).

Main body text set in Tw Cen MT Std Medium.
Typeface provided by Monotype Typography.

Library of Congress Cataloging-in-Publication Data

Names: Catarevas, Eve Nadel, 1957– author. | Peluso, Martina, illustrator.
Title: Rena Glickman, queen of judo / By Eve Nadel Catarevas ; Illustrated by Martina Peluso.
Description: Minneapolis, MN : Kar-Ben Publishing, [2022] | Audience: Ages 5–9 | Audience: Grades 2–3 | Summary: "Rena Glickman, known professionally as Rusty Kanokogi, was a poor Jewish girl who grew up to become the preeminent female judo master of her time" —Provided by publisher.
Identifiers: LCCN 2021014698 (print) | LCCN 2021014699 (ebook) | ISBN 9781728424309 | ISBN 9781728427973 (paperback) | ISBN 9781728444192 (ebook)
Subjects: LCSH: Kanokogi, Rusty 1935–2009—Juvenile literature. | Judo—Juvenile literature. | Judo for women—Juvenile literature.
Classification: LCC GV1113.K36 C38 2022 (print) | LCC GV1113.K36 (ebook) | DDC 796.815/2—dc23

LC record available at https://lccn.loc.gov/2021014698
LC ebook record available at https://lccn.loc.gov/2021014699

Manufactured in the United States of America
1-49300-49416-6/4/2021

RENA GLICKMAN, QUEEN OF JUDO

Eve Nadel Catarevas

Illustrated by Martina Peluso

KAR-BEN
PUBLISHING

In 1935, Coney Island was one of the most exciting neighborhoods in New York City. People came to swim, eat popcorn, gawk at rare animals, and enjoy thrilling rides. They came to have fun.

Coney Island was where feisty, redheaded Rena Glickman was born. Rena's life wasn't much fun. She lived in an apartment that was cramped and loud. Not even Shabbat brought quiet.

There was never enough money in the Glickman family.

Rena's parents didn't give her much, but they did give her a nickname, Rusty—after a stray neighborhood dog with red fur.

Her mother made a little money working at a hot dog stand. Rusty worked there too, peeling potatoes for french fries and selling cups of ice water after school.

Rena loved her brother, Charly. She wanted to be just like him. So when Charly lifted weights and did push-ups, so did Rusty. She became strong. That gave her the confidence to speak her mind, whether people wanted to hear what she had to say or not.

The Glickmans' neighbors disapproved of Rusty. "That girl's trouble. Always got to have her way. So stubborn and bossy and unladylike! Keep your distance," mothers warned their daughters.

Rusty went looking for friends. In rough neighborhoods like hers during the 1950s, teenagers sometimes formed street gangs. Rusty became the leader of a girls' gang. The gang members dressed alike and looked out for one another.

Sometimes they fought with rival gangs, so Rusty put her strength to use. She was always trying to improve her self-defense skills.

One day, a friend of Charly's showed Rusty a move he'd learned in a judo class at the YMCA. He weighed much less than Rusty, but before she knew it, he'd knocked her legs out from under her and flipped her like a pancake onto the floor. *THWAP!* Rusty sprang to her feet, amazed. She wanted to learn how to do that.

The next day, Rusty rushed to the YMCA and begged the judo instructor to let her join his class. He told her the class was for men only.

But Rusty kept coming back every day until he finally agreed to let her join.

The YMCA had no women's locker room, so Rusty changed clothes in the broom closet.

She worked harder than any of the men, arriving earlier and staying later.

She finally found a place where she could be herself, where no one told her to act more ladylike.

In judo, her toughness was accepted—even encouraged.

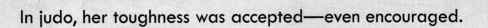

Rusty thought about judo all the time.

She thought about it while she washed the dishes. She thought about it at her job as a telephone operator. She dreamed about it in her sleep.

While waiting on the subway platform each
morning, she pressed her hands against a wall,
thrusting her body forward, trying to perfect a
throwing technique called O-*uchi-gari*.

She practiced foot sweeps called *De-ashi-harai* on
unsuspecting trash cans.

On the train, she did hundreds of leg-strengthening squats.

Fellow riders gave her strange looks and backed away. Rusty didn't care. She always said, "In life, you're either the hammer or the nail." Rusty had no intention of being the nail!

By her third year of training, Rusty had taken down half the men at the YMCA.

She decided it was time to compete in a tournament—
something no woman had ever done.

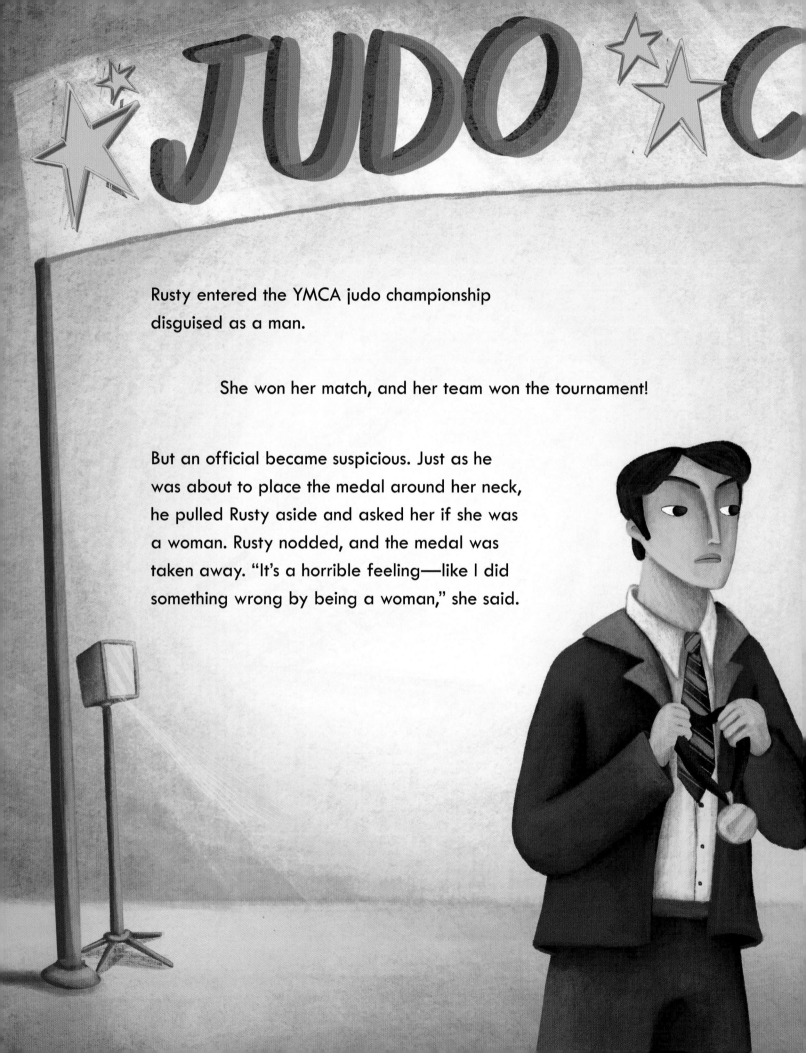

Rusty entered the YMCA judo championship disguised as a man.

She won her match, and her team won the tournament!

But an official became suspicious. Just as he was about to place the medal around her neck, he pulled Rusty aside and asked her if she was a woman. Rusty nodded, and the medal was taken away. "It's a horrible feeling—like I did something wrong by being a woman," she said.

Rusty didn't give up on competing. In 1962, she flew to Japan to study at the world-famous Kodokan, global headquarters of the judo community. She was the first woman allowed to train there, practicing nine hours a day.

There she met Ryohei Kanokogi—a judo, karate, and stick-fighting expert. As they trained together, they also fell in love.

Ryohei and Rusty left Japan for New York, where they got married and opened a training center near Rusty's old neighborhood. They devoted their lives to making women's judo a popular sport.

When men's judo became an Olympic sport in 1964, Rusty thought women's judo should be included too. She wrote thousands of letters to athletes, referees, politicians, and celebrities, asking for their support. She stormed into offices and made phone calls to anyone who would listen. She argued with members of athletic organizations who insisted that Americans weren't interested in watching women perform judo.

Rusty wouldn't back down. She started organizing women's judo competitions. In 1980, she used almost all her money to help pay for the first women's judo world championship. The event was a success, convincing many people that women's judo was an important and interesting sport.

Rusty's persistence paid off. In 1988, women's judo finally became an Olympic sport, with Rusty as the American team's coach.

For the rest of her life, Rusty continued to promote the sport she loved so much. She taught other women to believe in their abilities. She told all her students what she wished she'd been told as a child: "We're going to build on what you have, because you have a lot."

Author's Note

Rena "Rusty" Glickman Kanokogi (1935–2009) was the first woman to become a seventh-degree black belt in judo. She was inducted into the International Women's Sports Hall of Fame and the International Jewish Sports Hall of Fame. She also received the Order of the Rising Sun, bestowed on foreigners who have had a positive influence on Japanese society.

Rusty received recognition close to home as well. Fifty years after her very first tournament, the New York YMCA awarded Rusty the medal that she'd been forced to give up. After her death, a street in Coney Island, the New York City neighborhood where Rusty grew up, was named after her.

Without Rusty's tireless energy and unwavering belief in herself, women's judo and women's sports would not be what they are today. She inspired countless girls and women to dream, to compete, and to achieve.

Rusty with her mother in front of their house on Coney Island

Rusty Kanokogi, coach of the first United States Olympic Women's Judo Team, 1988

Rusty Kanokogi before demonstrating a judo throw at the Jangchung Gymnasium, Junggu District, Seoul, 1988 Seoul Summer Olympics